CHILDCARE
GURU

A SINGLE MOM'S JOURNEY TO BUILDING A 7-FIGURE BUSINESS FROM SCRATCH & A SUCCESS GUIDE TO LAUNCH AND SCALE YOUR CHILDCARE BUSINESS.

By:

Shekia James

Published by Live Limitless Media Group
Publishing@sierrarainge.com
info@livelimitlessmedia.com

Shekia James Contact Information:
Email: Mzdaycareguru@gmail.com
Website:Mzdaycareguru.com

Printed in the United States of America

ISBN: 9781952903502
Library of Congress Number: 2023920820

Dedication

I'd like to dedicate this book to my two sons Shandan and Eugene. You two have inspired me to pursue my goals everyday, consider me their superhero, you drive me to want to push forward. You make me feel like the sky is the limit. You are always inspiring me, holding me accountable, asking me how my day is…..

Acknowledgements

I would like to begin by giving a heartfelt thank you to my two incredible sons, who are the true inspiration behind this journey. Your curiosity, love, and unwavering support have been the foundation upon which I built my childcare business and the motivation behind writing this book. You both are my greatest teachers, and your joy and laughter remind me every day why I do what I do.

To my family and close friends, your constant encouragement has been a beacon of light on this journey. You have always believed in me, even when I doubted myself, and pushed me to share my experiences and knowledge with the world. Your belief in my mission to inspire others has been the driving force behind this book, and I am so grateful for your love and support.

A special thanks to my incredible publishing team at Live Limitless Media Group. Your expertise, dedication, and guidance have made this project come to life in a way I never imagined. Thank you for believing in this vision and helping me bring it to fruition.

I would also like to express my deepest gratitude to the families who trust me to care for their little ones. Your trust in me and my team is the highest honor, and I am privileged to play a role in nurturing and guiding your children. Thank you for being part of my journey.

To my community, your unwavering support has been invaluable. Your belief in the importance of quality childcare and your commitment to helping me grow my business have made all the difference. Together, we continue to create a place where children can flourish, and I am thankful for every opportunity to serve you.

And finally, to the little learners who inspire me every single day — your bright eyes, boundless curiosity, and ability to learn and grow remind me of why I am so passionate about what I do. You are the true heroes of this story, and it is for you that I continue to strive for excellence in everything I do.

Thank you all from the bottom of my heart.

Table of Contents

Introduction

In life, there are those who allow circumstances to shape their destiny, and then there are those who possess an unwavering will to win and allow their problems to push them towards success, promise and prosperity. Those who see challenges not as insurmountable roadblocks, but as opportunities for growth and transformation are the very people who turn lemons into lemonade and recognize the testimony that lives within each of life's tests. As a young single mother, my resilience was tested as I struggled to not only make ends meet, but to provide my boys with the early childhood learning experiences and education that would prepare them for a future of success.

Like so many parents, I experienced firsthand the frustrations and challenges of finding quality and affordable childcare for my boys. The overcrowded centers, disinterested staff, and soaring costs left me disheartened and yearning for a better alternative. It was in that moment of discontent that a spark of inspiration ignited within me, urging me to take matters into my own hands.

Driven by a deep desire to create a nurturing and educational environment for my own kids while making child care accessible to all, I embarked on a journey that would forever change the trajectory of my life. I decided to launch my own childcare business where I could incorporate, teach and impart the core values that I deemed to be most important in fostering growth, wellness and excellence in children. My vision went beyond simply providing a safe space for children; I wanted to develop a comprehensive curriculum that would empower and educate those from marginalized communities and inspire single mother's to pursue success and build wealth while also prioritizing their children's future.

I took the first steps towards building a childcare service that would redefine the standards of care and revolutionize opportunities for single mothers to transform their earning potential. Little did I know that this decision would propel me towards unprecedented success, catapulting my business to the realm of massive success and influence.

Today I own and operate a 7 figure childcare and consulting business where I'm able to leverage my 14 years of experience, a background in finance and banking with my passion for educating children to inspire the next generation of entrepreneurs and early childhood educators.

This book is not only a testament to my personal journey but also a guide for those aspiring to venture into the world of childcare. Within these pages, I will share my experiences, challenges, and triumphs, all while providing valuable insights and practical strategies to help you launch and scale your own childcare business.

Throughout the following chapters, we will explore the four essential competencies that have been instrumental in my own journey: community, care, compliance, and curriculum. Each of these competencies serves as a cornerstone for success, offering a multifaceted approach to building a thriving childcare service.

With a focus on "Community," we will delve into the importance of fostering strong relationships with parents, local organizations, and the broader community. I will share the transformative power of building a supportive network and the impact it can have on your business's growth.

"Caring" goes beyond the basic responsibilities of childcare; it encompasses the nurturing of young minds and hearts. In this chapter, I will delve into the essential components of creating a safe, stimulating, and inclusive environment where every child can thrive.

Navigating the world of regulations and compliance can be overwhelming, but in the "Compliance" portion of this book, I

3

will demystify the complexities and guide you through the necessary steps to ensure your business meets all legal requirements.

Lastly, we take a deep dive into the development of effective "Curriculum" where we will explore the transformative potential of designing a comprehensive and engaging curriculum that caters to the unique needs and abilities of the children in your care. I will share insights on fostering creativity, encouraging play-based learning, and embracing cultural sensitivity.

As you turn each page, be prepared to be inspired, empowered, and equipped with the knowledge and tools necessary to make a lasting impact in the lives of children and families. My story is a testament to the incredible possibilities that arise when passion, determination, and a genuine desire to make a difference collide.

In the chapters that follow, we will explore the depths of childcare entrepreneurship, uncovering the secrets to success and embracing the immense joy that comes from empowering young lives. Let my story be an example of what is possible when you establish a standard for excellence and when it does not exist, you decide to create it. Allow my pathway to success to be your guide, as we shape a future where all children receive the love, care, and educational foundation they deserve.

I wrote this book because I know firsthand the struggles of parenting without a partner. I know what it's like to want more for your child than what was accessible to you. I know what it's like to need to work to pay the bills and the cost of childcare exceeds your rate of pay. To every single mother committed to creating a better life for her children, and every person who holds a passion for children in their hearts and has a desire to make a positive impact in the lives of our youth, this book is for you. As you learn and implement the practical steps within this guide, you too can become a *Childcare Guru.*

If you picked up this book, you're committed to learning how to launch or scale your childcare business. Before we dive into my four core competencies of effective childcare with a standard of excellence, there are a few basic things that we need to cover. To begin, you need to decide what type of childcare business is right for you by discovering the various types of childcare models.

1. *Home care* -- A nanny or sitter cares for and supervises a child in the child's home. Not licensed by the state

2. *Day-care and child development centers* -- Programs designed to respond to the stages of physical, emotional, social and intellectual growth and behavior of infants and children. Licensed by the state

3. *Child care development home* -- A private residence for up to five children, with no more than two infants in the group. Licensed by the state

4. *Infant care center* -- A child development center that cares for infants and toddlers (children two years old or younger).

5. *Before- and after-school care* -- A program providing care for school-age children before and after the regular school day in a child development center or home.

6. *Satellite child development program* -- A private residence linked with a child development center or an agency that receives technical assistance and support, training, recruiting and placement.

7. *Nursery school* -- Usually a part-time preschool child development center operating during the school year.

For the purpose of this book, we are going to primarily focus on daycare and child development centers.

A Single Mom's Journey to Building a 7-Figure Business from Scratch

I never imagined that the seed for my childcare business would be planted in the most personal way — as a mother. Six months after my oldest son started daycare, I realized that the care he was receiving just wasn't what I expected or hoped for. As a parent, I wanted to ensure that my son was in an environment that not only took care of his basic needs but also nurtured his growth, education, and social development. Unfortunately, the daycare he attended lacked many of these essential elements.

The cleanliness of the facility wasn't up to my standards, the food they served wasn't nutritious, and the educational activities seemed minimal at best. What concerned me the most, though, was the lack of focus on socializing and ensuring that the children were interacting in ways that would benefit their emotional and cognitive development. As a mother, I felt that I could do better. And as a businesswoman-to-be, I knew I could offer something different.

It was this frustration, this desire for a higher standard of care, that led me to take a leap of faith and start my own daycare business. I had no business background at the time, but I knew that I could create an environment that was both nurturing and educational for children — just as I wanted for my own son. So, I decided to enroll in school to pursue a childcare certification. I studied hard, passed the necessary tests, and began the process of setting up my home daycare.

Opening a daycare from home wasn't easy, but it was one of the most rewarding decisions I ever made. Within 30 days of starting, my daycare was full. The demand was overwhelming, and I realized that there were many parents who felt the same way I did — they wanted higher quality care for their children. I worked tirelessly, pouring my heart and soul into providing the best care possible. As a single mother, I knew that I had to make it work not just for my son but for the families I was serving.

But while the home daycare was thriving, I knew I couldn't stop there. I was determined to grow and provide even more for the children and families that trusted me. About a year into my journey, I was able to find my first building — a true milestone in my business. This was a turning point, as it marked the shift from a small home operation to a legitimate childcare business. I continued to work relentlessly, using grassroots marketing and becoming deeply involved in my local community. I built relationships with parents, networked with local businesses, and even offered free parenting workshops. Every step I took helped my business grow and establish its place in the community.

As my daycare expanded, so did my financial success. The hard work, the long hours, and the sacrifices all paid off. I was able to purchase a million-dollar home, something I never imagined I'd achieve as a single mother. Not only had I built a thriving business, but I had also built a life I was proud of. I was able to provide for my son in a way that gave me pride and security. The journey wasn't without its challenges, but every obstacle I faced only strengthened my resolve to succeed.

Looking back, I realize that what began as a simple desire to provide better care for my son turned into a thriving childcare business that continues to impact the lives of many children and families. And while the financial success I've achieved is something I'm proud of, it's the impact on the children I've cared for and the families I've helped that gives me the most satisfaction.

This journey has shown me the importance of high-quality childcare and the significant role it plays in shaping the future of children. It's not just about providing a safe place for children to stay; it's about nurturing their development and preparing them for the future. As I look ahead, I'm even more determined to help others create quality childcare facilities that make a real difference — because I know firsthand how powerful a positive, enriching environment can be for a child.

In the following chapters, we'll explore the growing need for quality childcare facilities and why it's essential to meet that need with the highest standards of care. The demand is greater than ever, and the opportunity to build impactful businesses in the childcare space is vast. But to truly make a difference, we must understand what goes into creating not just a daycare, but a thriving, high-quality facility that meets the needs of both children and parents.

_____

_____

_____

_____

_____

_____

_____

_____

_____

_____

_____

_____

_____

_____

_____

_____

_____

_____

_____

_____

_____

_____

Chapter 1

Meeting the Growing Need: The Importance of Quality Childcare Facilities

The driving force behind the start of my business was the goal of solving a problem. In fact, entrepreneurship is all about recognizing a problem, creating a solution for the problem, creating demand around that solution and then getting people to pay you for it.

With the growing demand for women to gain willful employment, the demand for childcare services is steadily on the rise. Working mothers, whether in single- or two-parent households, constitute the fastest-growing demographic of the paid workforce.

In the ever-changing landscape of modern society, the need for quality childcare has become an increasingly vital concern for families and communities alike. As more and more parents, particularly mothers, step into the workforce, the demand for reliable, nurturing, and educational childcare facilities has reached unprecedented heights.

In recent decades, a significant shift in traditional gender roles has led to a surge in working mothers. The days of the stereotypical full-time mother and homemaker has changed and we are seeing a new reality where women are actively pursuing professional careers alongside their male counterparts. This societal evolution has placed greater responsibility on the childcare sector to provide the necessary support and care for children while their parents go to work. This demand for women to work creates massive opportunities for childcare facilities to exist and thrive.

High-quality childcare facilities play a fundamental role in shaping a child's early development. Early childhood is a critical period for cognitive, emotional, and social growth, and the environment in which children spend their formative years significantly influences their outcomes. Research consistently highlights the positive impact of quality childcare on a child's language skills, emotional intelligence, problem-solving abilities, and overall academic performance.

As a society, we have a collective responsibility to invest in the well-being and future of our children. By offering accessible and exceptional childcare facilities, we create an environment that fosters a love for learning, encourages curiosity, and nurtures each child's unique talents and interests. Children are the architects of our future, and it is our duty to equip them with the tools and experiences they need to become confident and capable individuals.

Working parents face the constant challenge of balancing their professional commitments with their responsibilities as caregivers. The availability of reliable and quality childcare facilities eases the burden on parents, enabling them to focus on their careers while knowing that their children are in safe and caring hands. Empowering parents with dependable childcare options contributes to greater job satisfaction and increased productivity in the workforce.

Access to quality child care is a critical factor in addressing disparities and inequality among different socioeconomic backgrounds. By offering equal opportunities for early education and development, we can bridge the gap between disadvantaged children and their more privileged peers. Investing in quality childcare for all children, regardless of their background, ensures that they have an equal chance to thrive and succeed.

The growing need for quality childcare facilities is undeniable, and it is a call to action for policymakers, communities, and entrepreneurs to come together to create a brighter future for our children. By providing exceptional childcare options, we invest not only in the present well-being of our children but also in the prosperity and strength of our society as a whole. The need for caring for the next generation of leaders is prevalent which means that you are able to enter an industry shaped by society's demand on women to work to earn a living while ensuring the safety and education of the little ones that they hold dear. Now that you have established the need for childcare, it's now important to carve out a niche so that you stand out and establish yourself in a sometimes saturated market.

To carve out a unique space in the childcare market, you must consider offering services that your competitors may have overlooked or aren't currently providing. For instance, if existing childcare centers in your area cater only to children aged three to five, you could explore offering care for newborns, infants, and one- to two-year-old toddlers. Alternatively, in addition to daily daycare services, you might consider providing after-school care for children between the ages of six and twelve.

When assessing the childcare services available in your community, consider the following questions:

1. What types of childcare are already present in the community?

2. Which age groups are being served, such as infants, toddlers, preschoolers, school-age children, or combinations of these?

3. Are there particular age groups with a higher demand for care than others?

4. What are the operating hours of existing centers?

5. What specific services do they offer, such as day care, night care, evening care, or after-school care?

6. How many childcare centers currently operate in the area, and where are they located?

7. Are there waiting lists for childcare services, indicating potential gaps in supply and demand?

8. Is there a need for additional centers in the same geographical area?

9. What services can you provide that aren't offered by other centers?

To gather information about the existing childcare programs in your community, consider the following steps:

1. Contact the licensing office at your local municipal center for insights into registered childcare facilities.

2. Reach out to the local day-care and referral agency to learn about available services and potential gaps.

3. Examine the Yellow Pages for additional childcare centers operating in your vicinity.

Regardless of the specific service you plan to provide, ensure that it meets the community's needs, aligns with children's interests, and promotes their development, including intellectual, social, emotional, and physical growth. Take the time to review all available options before finalizing the services you intend to offer, and ensure that your chosen approach will stand out as a valuable and unique addition to the childcare landscape.

PART ONE

Communication

It's almost impossible to have a conversation about childcare without placing an emphasis on community. Not only is it necessary to assess the childcare needs within the community you want to serve, but I want to take it a step further to assess the need for community childcare providers to come together to create a collective standard for care, compensation and compliance. While each facility may have its own niche, the idea of establishing a community standard across the board creates an atmosphere of cohesiveness and collaboration regarding the care of the children within a particular community.

Chapter 2

The Power of Effective Communication in Childcare

As a childcare leader and business owner, I have come to realize that effective communication is the heartbeat of a thriving childcare facility. From the way I communicate with my staff to how they engage with parents, each interaction plays a pivotal role in creating a warm, nurturing, and harmonious environment for the children in our care.

1. Fostering Communication Among Staff:

Within our childcare facility, open and clear communication among the team is the cornerstone of our success. As a leader, I believe in fostering an environment where each staff member feels heard, valued, and supported. Regular team meetings provide a platform for sharing ideas, addressing concerns, and celebrating successes. By encouraging open dialogue, we ensure that everyone's voice is heard, and we collectively work towards providing the best care possible for the children.

2. Engaging and Supporting Parents:

Effective communication with parents is equally crucial in building trust and maintaining strong relationships. We follow my "sunset policy," ensuring that parents feel connected with the childcare facility every day. If a parent doesn't see me during morning drop-offs, they can be sure they will see me during afternoon pickups, providing a personal touch to our communication and reaffirming our commitment to their child's well-being.

3. Building Connections Among Children:

In a childcare setting, communication goes beyond the exchange of words. We emphasize the importance of non-verbal communication and actively encourage positive interactions among the children. By fostering a culture of empathy and respect, we create an environment where children feel safe and encouraged to express themselves, fostering their social and emotional development.

4. Embracing Technology to Enhance Care:

In today's digital age, technology has become a valuable ally in enhancing childcare services and communication. We have implemented an innovative app that allows my staff and I to engage in high-touch communication with parents throughout the day. With this app, we provide real-time updates every two hours, complete with pictures and messages, offering parents a glimpse into their child's day and fostering a sense of connectedness, and trust.

5. Empowering Parent Involvement:

Our commitment to communication extends beyond the walls of our childcare facility. We actively involve parents in their child's development journey, soliciting their input and ideas. Regular parent-teacher conferences provide a space for discussing progress, milestones, and addressing any concerns. We view parents as integral partners in their child's education, and their involvement significantly enriches the learning experience.

6. Nurturing a Culture of Collaboration:

Effective communication not only happens vertically but also horizontally within our team. My staff members collaborate with one another, share ideas, and support each other in their daily responsibilities. By fostering a culture of collaboration, we create a positive and harmonious atmosphere that directly benefits the children under our care.

I prioritize open, transparent, and compassionate communication with my staff, parents, and the children we serve.

By embracing technology as a powerful communication tool, we have transformed the way we engage with parents, keeping them closely connected to their child's experiences throughout the day. Through the power of communication, we have cultivated a loving and supportive environment that nurtures each child's growth and development, ensuring they flourish in our care while allowing parents to have access to their child's learning experience.

Action Steps to Create a Communication Standard and Policy for Your Childcare Business:

1. Assess Current Communication Practices:

- Evaluate your current communication methods with staff, parents, and children.

- Identify any gaps or areas that need improvement in your communication processes.

2. Define Clear Communication Goals:

- Determine the key objectives of your communication policy, such as enhancing parent involvement, promoting staff collaboration, and ensuring child safety.

3. Involve Your Team:

– Engage your staff in discussions about communication needs and challenges they face.

– Encourage feedback and ideas to ensure a collaborative approach.

4. Research Communication Tools and Platforms:

– Explore various communication tools and platforms, such as apps, email, and newsletters.

– Consider their features, ease of use, and compatibility with your childcare business.

5. Establish Communication Channels:

– Determine which communication channels will be used for staff-to-staff, staff-to-parent, and parent-to-staff interactions.

– Clearly outline when each channel should be used and for what purposes.

6. Create a Parent Handbook:

– Develop a comprehensive parent handbook that outlines your communication policy, including preferred methods of communication and response times.

7. Set Response Time Expectations:

– Establish reasonable response time expectations for all communication channels.

– Clearly communicate these expectations to staff and parents.

8. Develop Child-Specific Communication Plans:

– Create individualized communication plans for children with specific needs or health considerations.

– Ensure that all staff members are aware of these plans and follow them consistently.

9. Provide Communication Training for Staff:

– Conduct training sessions to educate staff on effective communication techniques.

– Address best practices for interacting with parents and maintaining professionalism.

10. Implement Technology Solutions:

– Choose and implement the communication tools and platforms that align with your goals and preferences.

– Train staff and parents on how to use these tools effectively.

Checklist for Creating a Communication Standard and Policy:

☐ Evaluate current communication practices and identify areas for improvement.

☐ Define clear communication goals for your childcare business.

☐ Engage your staff in discussions and gather feedback on communication needs.

☐ Research and select appropriate communication tools and platforms.

☐ Determine communication channels for staff-to-staff, staff-to-parent, and parent-to-staff interactions.

☐ Create a parent handbook that includes your communication policy and expectations.

☐ Set response time expectations for different communication channels.

☐ Develop individualized communication plans for children with specific needs.

☐ Provide communication training for staff to enhance their communication skills.

☐ Implement selected technology solutions and ensure proper training for staff and parents.

☐ Regularly review and update your communication policy as needed to meet changing needs.

By following these action steps and using the checklist, aspiring childcare providers can establish an effective communication standard and policy that fosters a positive and supportive environment for staff, parents, and the children in their care.

The Power of Effective Communication in Childcare

As a childcare leader and business owner, I have come to realize that effective communication is the heartbeat of a thriving childcare facility. From the way I communicate with my staff to how they engage with parents, each interaction plays a pivotal role in creating a warm, nurturing, and harmonious environment for the children in our care. The way we communicate sets the tone for everything in the facility—from the relationships we build with parents to the comfort and security the children feel as they spend their days with us.

When I first started in the childcare industry, I quickly learned that communication wasn't just about talking—it was about listening, understanding, and responding with empathy. The words we say matter, but how we say them and how we listen is just as crucial. This realization hit home one particular day when I had a situation with a parent that I knew could have easily turned into a conflict.

It started with a concerned mother who came to me in a panic. Her daughter had been with us for several months, and everything seemed to be going well. However, this day, her mother had picked her up and noticed something unusual. Her daughter was slightly withdrawn, didn't seem like herself, and was reluctant to share anything about her day. Naturally, the mother was concerned.

Now, as a business owner, there's always pressure to maintain a positive image, and the first instinct could be to quickly offer explanations and assurances, trying to smooth over the situation. However, I knew this moment was about more than just answering her questions. It was an opportunity for me to demonstrate the kind of communication that builds trust and fosters meaningful relationships with the parents who entrust us with their children every day.

I took a deep breath and calmly sat down with the mother, giving her my full attention. I didn't jump to conclusions or immediately try to provide answers. Instead, I asked her to walk me through what she had noticed and how her daughter had been acting at home. As she spoke, I listened intently, validating her feelings. I reflected her concerns back to her: "It sounds like you're worried because your daughter seems more reserved than usual today. I can understand why that would make you uneasy."

Through active listening, I not only gained a better understanding of the mother's perspective, but I also communicated that her feelings were valid, and that we were partners in ensuring her daughter's well-being. After a few moments of discussion, I offered some possible explanations for her daughter's behavior and reassured her that we'd be monitoring the situation closely. By the end of the conversation, the mother felt heard and supported. This one conversation helped to strengthen the relationship with this parent, and the concern she had initially felt turned into a sense of partnership.

That day, I learned the true power of effective communication. It wasn't about having all the answers immediately; it was about fostering a two-way dialogue that made both the parent and child feel understood. It was about creating a space where concerns could be shared and resolved in a constructive way. It reinforced the importance of transparency, empathy, and patience.

In a childcare setting, where emotions can run high and concerns are always at the forefront of parents' minds, communication is key. But effective communication is also a two-way street. It's not just about the owner or the staff communicating with the parents—it's about creating an environment where everyone feels heard. That includes the children.

I once observed an interaction between one of our teachers and a child that perfectly exemplified the importance of listening. This particular child had been struggling with separation anxiety when dropped off in the morning. Every day, she would cling to her mother, her eyes full of tears, and would only calm down after her mother had left. While this is a common stage in early childhood, it was challenging for both the child and the staff to witness.

One morning, the teacher noticed that the child seemed to be a little more reserved than usual, even before the mother arrived. Instead of simply going through the motions and starting the routine, the teacher took a moment to get down to the child's level and engage her. She asked open-ended questions: "How are you feeling today? Is there something you want to talk about?" The teacher didn't rush her or try to push her into the classroom too quickly. She simply listened, giving the child the time and space to express herself.

After a few moments, the child, a little hesitant at first, opened up and said that she was feeling nervous because her mother had to leave for a work trip that day. The teacher reassured her gently, "It's okay to miss your mommy. We're going to have a fun day, and I'll be here to help you feel better." By acknowledging the child's feelings and giving her a safe space to express them, the teacher communicated that her emotions were valid. From that moment on, the child's separation anxiety began to decrease because she knew she had someone who would listen and support her.

The power of communication goes beyond just resolving issues; it's about building relationships that foster trust and understanding. It's about creating an environment where everyone, from the children to the parents to the staff, feels valued and supported. Effective communication allows us to work together to address challenges, celebrate successes, and continuously improve the care we provide.

As childcare providers, it's easy to underestimate the profound impact our words can have on the children and families we serve. Communication shapes the culture of our facility, sets expectations, and establishes an atmosphere of respect and care.

When done right, it can transform not only individual relationships but the entire culture of our childcare business.

Effective communication is more than just a skill—it's the foundation upon which everything else is built. It's the bridge between parents and providers, staff and children, and between the values we hold and the way we run our facilities. In the following chapters, we will explore the practical ways to implement effective communication strategies that will elevate your childcare business, foster stronger relationships, and ensure that you're meeting the needs of every child in your care. Whether it's through improving your communication with parents, your staff, or the children themselves, mastering this skill will be the key to creating a thriving, successful childcare environment.

PART TWO

Care

Chapter 3

Empowering Effective Care: Essential Tools for Your Childcare Business

E nsuring effective care within a childcare business requires a comprehensive toolkit that encompasses safety protocols, valuable resources, and thoughtful considerations of the community's demographic. As an aspiring childcare provider, equipping yourself with these essential tools will not only foster a nurturing environment for the children but also instill confidence in parents, making your childcare business a trusted cornerstone of the community.

1. Safety Protocols: The Cornerstone of Trust

Safety is paramount when it comes to caring for children. Develop robust safety protocols that encompass all aspects of childcare operations. This includes thorough background checks for staff, adherence to child-to-staff ratios, emergency preparedness plans, and rigorous cleanliness and hygiene practices. Regularly review and update these protocols to ensure that your childcare business remains a safe haven for the children in your care.

2. Nourishing Growing Minds: Food Programs and Nutrition

Nutrition plays a vital role in supporting a child's growth and development. Partner with reputable food programs that offer well-balanced meals to cater to children's varying dietary needs. Emphasize the importance of healthy eating habits and age-appropriate nutrition to instill lifelong habits that promote overall well-being.

3. Setting Tuition Rates: Balancing Affordability and Quality

Developing tuition rates based on the community's demographic is a delicate balance. Consider the cost of providing quality care, including staff salaries, resources, and facility maintenance, while also taking into account the economic circumstances of the families you serve. Offering flexible payment options or exploring subsidized programs can help ensure accessibility to families from diverse backgrounds.

4. Building Relationships: A Community-Centric Approach

Create an open and collaborative atmosphere by building strong relationships within the community. Engage in open dialogues with parents to understand their needs and concerns, and involve them in decision-making processes. Forge partnerships with local organizations, schools, and businesses to expand resources and enrich the children's experiences.

5. Professional Development: Nurturing Your Team

Invest in the continuous growth of your staff through professional development opportunities. Provide training sessions that enhance their caregiving skills, including child development, behavior management, and effective communication techniques. A well-trained and motivated team will deliver exceptional care and contribute to a positive reputation for your childcare business.

6. Engaging Curriculum: Fostering Holistic Development

Design a curriculum that promotes holistic development, encompassing cognitive, social, emotional, and physical aspects. Incorporate play-based learning, hands-on activities, and age-appropriate challenges that encourage children's curiosity and creativity. Tailor the curriculum to meet the diverse needs and interests of the children in your care.

By embracing these essential tools, you will lay a solid foundation for effective care within your childcare business. Safety protocols and nutritious food programs create a secure and nurturing environment, while community-centric approaches and well-balanced tuition rates foster a sense of trust and accessibility. Investing in your staff's professional development and implementing an engaging curriculum ensures that your childcare business becomes a beacon of quality care and a cherished asset to the community you serve.

Action Steps to Create a Care Standard and Policy for Your Childcare Business:

1. Define Your Philosophy and Values:

- Establish the core philosophy and values that will guide your childcare business.

- Clearly define your commitment to providing a nurturing, safe, and stimulating environment for the children in your care.

2. Research and Understand Regulations:

- Familiarize yourself with the childcare regulations and licensing requirements in your area.

- Ensure that your care standard aligns with these legal guidelines.

3. Involve Your Staff:

- Engage your staff in discussions about the care standard and policy.

- Encourage their input and feedback to create a collaborative approach.

4. Develop Clear Guidelines:

- Outline the daily routines, expectations, and guidelines for staff interactions with children.

- Address topics such as meal times, nap schedules, hygiene practices, and play-based learning activities.

5. Establish Safety Protocols:

- Develop comprehensive safety protocols, including emergency procedures and health and hygiene practices.

- Ensure that staff members are well-trained to handle emergency situations.

6. Create Parent Communication Guidelines:

- Set clear communication guidelines for interacting with parents.

- Establish regular communication methods to keep parents informed about their child's progress and well-being.

7. Implement Staff Training:

- Provide comprehensive training for all staff members on the care standard and policy.

- Ensure that they understand and adhere to the established guidelines.

8. Conduct Regular Assessments:

- Regularly assess the effectiveness of your care standard and policy.

- Seek feedback from parents and staff to identify areas for improvement.

9. Establish a Continuous Improvement Process:

- Develop a plan for continuous improvement based on feedback and assessments.

- Make necessary adjustments to enhance the quality of care provided.

Checklist for Creating a Care Standard and Policy for Your Childcare Business:

☐ Define the philosophy and values that will guide your childcare business.

☐ Familiarize yourself with the childcare regulations and licensing requirements in your area.

☐ Involve your staff in discussions and gather their input for the care standard and policy.

☐ Outline clear guidelines for daily routines, interactions with children, and learning activities.

☐ Develop comprehensive safety protocols, including emergency procedures and health practices.

☐ Establish communication guidelines for interacting with parents and keeping them informed.

☐ Provide staff training on the care standard and policy to ensure understanding and adherence.

☐ Regularly assess the effectiveness of your care standard and policy through feedback and assessments.

☐ Develop a continuous improvement plan based on feedback and assessments to enhance care quality.

By following these action steps and using the checklist, you can establish a care standard and policy that promotes a nurturing, safe, and stimulating environment for the children in their care. This comprehensive approach will not only meet regulatory requirements but also foster trust and confidence among parents, setting your childcare business up for success.

Essential Tools for Your Childcare Business

The quality of care provided in childcare facilities is largely determined by the tools and systems in place to support both caregivers and children. While it's easy to think that the most important aspect of childcare is simply the love and attention given to the children, the reality is that effective care requires a well-organized approach supported by essential tools—both physical and digital. A facility that lacks the right tools can struggle to provide the high standards of care parents expect.

Take, for example, a case from a well-known early childhood education facility in Seattle that was facing numerous operational and communication challenges. **Bright Futures Childcare**, a thriving center with 50+ children enrolled, had built a reputation for being a nurturing and caring environment. However, despite their excellent intentions, they faced challenges in maintaining consistent care, communicating effectively with parents, and managing day-to-day operations efficiently.

The Challenges

Bright Futures had a strong team of passionate educators and caregivers, but there were significant hurdles that hindered the overall effectiveness of the center. The staff was overburdened with administrative tasks, lesson planning was done manually with paper, and the center lacked a central communication platform for parent updates. As a result, staff were spending too much time on paperwork, and many parents felt they were not receiving enough communication about their child's daily experiences or developmental progress.

One of the biggest challenges was the issue of consistency. With multiple caregivers working in different rooms and shifts, there was no clear system for tracking children's individual progress or communicating about specific needs. This meant that staff might not have all the information they needed to provide the best care. For example, a child who was struggling with a mild form of separation anxiety might be met with confusion or a lack of support by different caregivers, leading to unnecessary distress.

Additionally, parents often expressed frustration at not being informed about their child's day in real-time. They received daily updates, but these were often vague, and the information did not give them a full picture of their child's activities, mood, or progress.

The Solution: Implementing Essential Tools

Recognizing the need for improvement, the owner of Bright Futures decided to invest in several key tools that would empower the staff, streamline operations, and improve communication. The first step was adopting a digital childcare management system, which included lesson planning, child tracking, and a parent communication app all in one.

This new system allowed caregivers to track each child's development in real time, noting milestones, challenges, and behavior patterns. By documenting observations digitally, the staff could quickly access and share important information with each other, making sure all caregivers were on the same page. The system also allowed teachers to share personalized daily reports with parents through the app, complete with photos and updates on their child's activities.

With a centralized system in place, Bright Futures was able to ensure that each child received individualized attention.

Caregivers could track behavioral patterns, learning progress, and emotional development, making it easier to provide tailored support. For example, a child who was struggling with communication could have a specific, individualized plan designed to address their needs, which all staff could follow, ensuring consistency throughout the day.

The parent communication app proved to be an invaluable tool. Parents were no longer left wondering how their child was doing throughout the day. They could see updates in real time, receive photos, and ask questions directly through the app. This direct communication built trust and allowed parents to stay connected with their child's day-to-day life. For instance, one parent noticed a change in their child's mood and was able to message the staff immediately, asking for more details. The staff, who had already documented the child's behavior, were able to provide an immediate response and adjust the child's care accordingly. This responsiveness not only helped address the parent's concern but also reinforced a sense of partnership and trust.

Streamlining Operations with Technology

In addition to improving communication, Bright Futures also implemented an employee scheduling system. This tool allowed caregivers to sign up for shifts, track their hours, and ensure that staffing levels were adequate at all times. With the increase in enrollment and the growing demand for quality childcare, this system was crucial for avoiding understaffing and ensuring that children were always supervised by qualified caregivers.

The scheduling tool also allowed the center's management to track staff hours and performance in a way that helped reduce burnout. With the ability to monitor workloads and track time off requests, Emily, the owner, could ensure that staff had adequate breaks and were not working beyond their capacity. This system played a large role in reducing turnover and boosting staff morale, as employees felt more supported and appreciated.

The Results: Positive Change

The tools Bright Futures implemented had an immediate and noticeable impact. Within just a few months, both staff and parents reported significant improvements. Teachers were able to spend less time on administrative tasks and more time focusing on the children. The ability to quickly access information on a child's development allowed for more effective interventions and ensured that each child's needs were being met consistently.

Parents, who had been frustrated by the lack of communication, now felt fully engaged in their child's day. They were able to provide valuable input and received the kind of personalized attention they had been hoping for. The daily updates became more detailed, and parents were able to see their child's growth in a way that was tangible and reassuring.

Staff turnover decreased as well, largely due to the improved communication and scheduling tools. Teachers felt supported, and they had the resources needed to provide the best care. The sense of community within the center grew stronger as staff and parents worked more closely together, sharing a common goal: to provide the highest quality of care for the children.

The transformation at Bright Futures Childcare underscores the importance of having the right tools in place to deliver effective care. By implementing systems for communication, lesson planning, and staff management, the center was able to streamline its operations and improve the quality of care provided. For any childcare business, empowering staff with the right tools isn't just a luxury—it's a necessity. When your team is equipped with the right resources, they can focus on what matters most: the children. And when parents are kept in the loop and have access to real-time updates, they feel more connected and confident in the care their child is receiving.

The right tools can make all the difference in creating a childcare environment that is not only efficient but nurturing. Whether it's through digital systems, improved communication strategies, or staff empowerment, the tools you choose to implement will have a lasting impact on the success of your business and the wellbeing of the children in your care.

Chapter 4

Expanding your earning potential as a childcare provider: Maximizing Capacity and Building Value

The potential to expand your earning capacity is directly tied to several key factors. By leveraging your facilities and resources effectively, you can tap into new opportunities for growth and success. In this chapter, we will explore various strategies to expand your earning potential, taking into account your staff capacity, building size, demographic income, number of children, location, extra-curricular activities offered, and the rates of other facilities in the area.

1. Staff Capacity: Empower Your Team for Growth

Your staff capacity plays a crucial role in expanding your childcare business's earning potential. Invest in training and professional development to equip your staff with the skills and knowledge to provide top-notch care. A well-trained and motivated team not only ensures high-quality service but also enables you to accommodate more children, thereby increasing your earning potential.

2. Building Size: Utilize Space Efficiently

Make the most of your building's layout and design to optimize your earning potential. Consider creating multi-functional spaces that can accommodate different age groups or offer diverse activities. By utilizing your space efficiently, you can serve more children and cater to various age-specific needs, attracting a broader client base.

3. Demographic Income: Tailor Services to Meet Diverse Needs

Understanding the income demographics of your target audience is essential for expanding your earning potential. Consider offering flexible payment options or part-time care services to cater to families with varying financial capacities. By tailoring your services to meet the diverse needs of your community, you can attract a wider range of clientele.

4. Number of Children: Striking the Right Balance

While increasing the number of children in your care can boost your earning potential, it's crucial to strike the right balance. Ensuring adequate staff-to-child ratios and maintaining high-quality care are paramount. Focus on achieving sustainable growth that doesn't compromise the quality of care provided.

5. Location: Leverage Your Surroundings

Your childcare facility's location can be a powerful asset in expanding your earning potential. If you are situated in a densely populated area or near businesses with working parents, market your convenience as a selling point. Additionally, consider partnering with nearby organizations to offer after-school programs or holiday camps, further maximizing your earning potential.

6. Extra-Curricular Activities: Add Value to Your Services

Offering extra-curricular activities can set your childcare facility apart from competitors and increase your earning potential. Consider incorporating educational programs, arts and crafts, music lessons, or physical activities that appeal to parents seeking comprehensive and enriching care for their children.

7. Rate Comparison and Value Proposition: Strive for Competitive Excellence

Research the rates of other childcare facilities in your area to stay competitive. However, rather than engaging in a price war, focus on creating a unique value proposition. Highlight the strengths of your facility, such as high-quality care, personalized attention, innovative programs, and a nurturing environment, to justify your rates and attract discerning parents seeking the best for their children.

By strategically aligning your staff capacity, building size, demographic income, number of children, location, extra-curricular activities, and rates, you can unlock new opportunities for expanding your earning potential as a childcare provider. Ultimately, by providing exceptional care and continuously striving for excellence, you will earn the trust and loyalty of parents, solidifying your position as a leading childcare facility in your community.

Action Steps to Expand Earning Potential and Scale Your Childcare Business:

1. Conduct Market Research:

- Research the local childcare market to identify demand, competition, and potential gaps in services.

- Gather data on the demographics and income levels of the community you aim to serve.

2. Define Your Unique Value Proposition:

- Identify what sets your childcare facility apart from competitors.

– Develop a clear and compelling value proposition that highlights the unique benefits of your services.

3. Enhance Staff Capacity and Expertise:

– Invest in staff training and professional development to elevate the quality of care provided.

– Consider hiring additional qualified staff to increase capacity and accommodate more children.

4. Optimize Facility Space and Layout:

– Evaluate your building's layout to maximize space utilization and accommodate more children comfortably.

– Create multi-functional areas to cater to diverse age groups and offer various activities.

5. Expand Services and Extra-Curricular Activities:

– Introduce new educational programs, enrichment activities, and extra-curricular options to attract parents seeking comprehensive care.

– Consider partnering with local businesses or organizations to offer specialized classes or events.

6. Offer Flexible Payment Options:

– Provide flexible payment plans or part-time care options to accommodate families with varying financial capacities.

– Consider accepting government subsidies or offering scholarships to increase accessibility.

7. Strategically Adjust Tuition Rates:

– Conduct a thorough cost analysis to determine appropriate tuition rates.

– Consider setting competitive rates while ensuring they align with the high-quality care and services you provide.

8. Establish Effective Marketing Strategies:

– Develop a comprehensive marketing plan to promote your childcare business.

– Utilize digital marketing, social media, local advertising, and community outreach to reach potential clients.

9. Nurture Positive Parent Relationships:

– Prioritize open and effective communication with parents to build trust and loyalty.

– Encourage parent involvement and feedback to continually improve services.

Checklist for Expanding Earning Potential and Scaling Your Childcare Business:

☐ Conducted thorough market research on the local childcare market and demographics.

☐ Defined a unique value proposition that highlights the strengths of your childcare facility.

☐ Invested in staff training and professional development to enhance the quality of care.

☐ Evaluated and optimized your facility's space and layout to accommodate more children comfortably.

☐ Introduced new educational programs, enrichment activities, or extra-curricular options to attract parents seeking comprehensive care.

☐ Offered flexible payment options or part-time care to accommodate families with varying financial capacities.

☐ Strategically adjusted tuition rates to align with the value of your services while remaining competitive.

☐ Developed a comprehensive marketing plan to promote your childcare business effectively.

☐ Prioritized open and effective communication with parents to build trust and foster positive relationships.

By following these action steps and using the checklist, you can create a solid foundation for expanding their earning potential and scaling their business successfully. Remember, consistent dedication to providing exceptional care and continuous improvement will contribute to the long-term growth and success of your childcare facility.

PART THREE

Curriculum

Chapter 5

Empowering Effective Care Through Curriculum Development

Curriculum development in early childhood education is much more than just selecting activities and themes for the day. It's about creating a learning environment that nurtures children's cognitive, social, emotional, and physical development in a way that aligns with their individual needs and interests. An effective curriculum sets the foundation for children to learn essential skills while also fostering creativity, curiosity, and a love of learning.

When I first started my childcare business, I quickly realized the importance of having a structured yet flexible curriculum in place. While play and exploration are key components of early childhood learning, I knew that providing an intentional, thoughtfully crafted curriculum was crucial to helping the children in my care develop to their full potential. However, designing a curriculum that works requires careful thought, planning, and an understanding of child development principles.

In this chapter, we will explore the critical elements of an effective curriculum, and you'll have the opportunity to develop your own personalized curriculum for your childcare setting. We'll dive into practical tools, real-life examples, and interactive prompts that will guide you in developing an enriching learning experience for the children in your care.

Let's consider the story of **Bright Beginnings Childcare**, a center in Portland that was facing challenges in providing consistent and high-quality learning experiences for children. The facility had a team of passionate educators, but the curriculum was outdated and lacked coherence. The center's management team realized that in order to meet the developmental needs of the children and stay competitive in the childcare market, they needed to update their curriculum.

The staff at Bright Beginnings started by analyzing the needs of the children they served, evaluating their age groups, developmental stages, and the unique strengths of each child. They recognized that many of the children in their care were at different stages in terms of language skills, motor development, and social abilities. This realization prompted them to look for ways to incorporate flexibility into their curriculum, ensuring that each child's individual needs were met.

One of the most powerful changes they made was introducing a **thematic approach to learning**. The staff began to focus on topics or themes each week—such as "Animal Kingdom," "Weather Wonders," and "The Big Family"—that sparked curiosity in the children. Each theme included hands-on activities that promoted learning in all areas: from science experiments to art projects, from language-building exercises to social skills activities.

For example, during their "Animal Kingdom" week, the children learned about different animals, their habitats, and characteristics. They engaged in a variety of activities such as creating animal masks, drawing their favorite animals, and even observing live animals in the classroom with a special guest. This thematic approach helped to engage the children, develop their cognitive skills, and encourage emotional expression through creative play.

By focusing on thematic, child-centered learning, Bright Beginnings created an environment where children felt safe, engaged, and excited to learn. The teachers embraced the idea that curriculum doesn't just consist of structured lessons—it's about creating experiences that foster growth and curiosity.

Building Your Own Effective Curriculum

Developing an effective curriculum for early childhood education doesn't have to be daunting. The key is to integrate the right balance of structure, creativity, and child-driven learning. As you build your curriculum, keep these core principles in mind:

1. **Developmentally Appropriate Practices**

   Your curriculum should be tailored to the developmental needs of the children in your care. Understanding child development is crucial to creating a curriculum that aligns with their capabilities and challenges them at the right level. Ensure that your activities are engaging and achievable for their age group.

2. **Hands-on Learning**

   Early childhood education thrives when children engage in hands-on learning experiences. Young children learn best by doing, exploring, and interacting with their environment. Incorporating sensory activities—such as playing with sand, water, clay, or building blocks—stimulates their cognitive and motor development.

3. **Inclusivity and Flexibility**

   Every child is unique, with their own strengths, challenges, and learning styles. Create a curriculum that is flexible and inclusive, offering opportunities for differentiation to meet the needs of all children. Whether it's modifying an activity to cater to a child's individual learning style or offering different levels of difficulty, be sure your curriculum can adapt to the diverse needs of your classroom.

4. **A Focus on Social and Emotional Development**

Early childhood is a time when children develop important social and emotional skills. Your curriculum should encourage collaboration, empathy, and communication. Provide opportunities for children to work in groups, share with peers, and practice problem-solving in social contexts.

At **Canvas Academy**, the curriculum was designed with one core mission in mind: to expose early learners to expanded possibilities for the future. I believe that introducing children to career opportunities and instilling the spirit of excellence and community impact from an early age is crucial for their development.

My curriculum at Canvas Academy emphasizes the power of **imagination**. Early childhood is a time when children's imaginations are at their peak, and I wanted to foster that creativity while exposing them to a wide range of careers and opportunities. By presenting young children with the idea that they can dream big and pursue a variety of career paths, I'm encouraging them to think outside the box and see the world as a place full of possibilities.

I believe in the importance of **instilling the spirit of excellence**. From a young age, children should be encouraged to do their best, strive for greatness, and take pride in their work. This not only sets them up for academic success, but also teaches them the value of hard work and perseverance.

I wanted to create a curriculum that emphasizes **community impact**. Children need to understand that their actions, no matter how small, can have a positive impact on the world around them. By incorporating community-based projects and discussions into the curriculum, I help children recognize their role in society and instill in them a sense of responsibility and empathy.

This philosophy shapes everything in the curriculum—from the activities we plan to the discussions we have. It's about helping children build a foundation for their future, one where they can envision themselves as leaders, creators, and changemakers.

Now that you've considered the principles of effective curriculum, it's time to start developing your own plan. Follow these steps to begin creating a curriculum that aligns with your childcare setting's values and meets the developmental needs of the children in your care.

1. **Assess the Needs of Your Children**

   Take some time to reflect on the children in your classroom. What are their current developmental stages? Are there specific skills or areas that need more focus? Use observations, discussions with parents, and your knowledge of child development to create a clear picture of their needs.

2. **Choose a Thematic Approach**

   Based on the interests and needs of your children, select a theme or topic that will guide your lessons for the upcoming weeks. Make sure the theme is broad enough to cover various learning areas, from science to art to language development. Think about what will excite and engage the children.

3. **Create a Weekly Schedule of Activities**

   Plan daily activities that align with your theme. For example, if your theme is "The Animal Kingdom," your schedule could include:

   o **Monday:** Storytime with animal books

   o **Tuesday:** Crafting animal masks

   o **Wednesday:** Animal song and dance

     o **Thursday:** Outdoor exploration (e.g., visit to a zoo or nature walk)

     o **Friday:** Show and tell (children share their favorite animal)

4. **Incorporate Learning Areas**

Ensure your activities cover key areas of development:

     o **Cognitive:** Puzzles, matching games, or science experiments

     o **Social-Emotional:** Group projects, role-playing, cooperative games

     o **Language:** Storytelling, songs, conversations

     o **Physical:** Outdoor play, sensory activities, motor skill development

5. **Evaluate and Reflect**

After each week, reflect on what worked well and what could be improved. Were the children engaged? Did they meet the learning goals? Make adjustments to your curriculum based on feedback and observation.

Curriculum Development Checklist

Use the following checklist to ensure that your curriculum is comprehensive and well-rounded:

☐ **Developmentally Appropriate**: Activities are suitable for the children's age and developmental stage.

☐ **Engaging and Fun**: The curriculum includes a variety of interactive and hands-on activities.

☐ **Inclusive**: Adjustments are made to accommodate diverse learning styles and needs.

☐ **Balanced**: A good mix of cognitive, social-emotional, language, and physical development.

☐ **Thematic**: The curriculum follows a central theme that is relevant and engaging.

☐ **Evaluative**: Regular assessments and reflections to adjust the curriculum as needed.

_____

_____

_____

_____

_____

_____

_____

_____

_____

_____

_____

_____

_____

_____

_____

_____

_____

_____

_____

_____

_____

_____

_____

_____

_____

_____

PART FOUR

Compliance

Chapter 6

Compliance in Childcare: The Foundation of Trust and Quality

Compliance is a word that many childcare providers may find intimidating, but it is one of the most important aspects of running a successful and sustainable childcare business. Ensuring that your facility meets all local, state, and federal regulations is not only a legal requirement but also a critical part of building trust with parents, staff, and the community.

As a childcare provider, the safety, well-being, and development of the children in your care should always be your top priority. Compliance ensures that you are upholding the highest standards of care, protecting children from harm, and operating a business that is transparent, ethical, and accountable.

In this chapter, we will explore the significance of compliance in the childcare industry, the steps to maintain adherence to regulatory standards, and practical tools that can help you stay organized and informed. We'll also address the long-term benefits of compliance, such as building a positive reputation and maintaining strong relationships with families.

Compliance in the childcare industry refers to adhering to a wide array of legal and regulatory requirements that govern the care and education of children. These regulations vary depending on your location, the size of your facility, and the age group of the children in your care, but they generally cover areas such as:

- **Health and Safety Standards**: Ensuring the physical safety of children, such as proper building safety, fire drills, and sanitation.

- **Staff Qualifications and Training**: Ensuring that staff members are appropriately trained, certified, and qualified to care for children.

- **Child-to-Staff Ratios**: Maintaining proper ratios of children to staff to ensure adequate supervision and individualized care.

- **Curriculum Standards**: Aligning your curriculum with state-approved guidelines for early childhood education.

- **Parental Rights and Involvement**: Ensuring that parents have access to relevant information about their child's development and that their rights are respected.

- **Licensing and Inspections**: Meeting the necessary licensing requirements and passing inspections by local regulatory bodies.

A Case Study: Sunshine Early Learning Center

Let's look at the example of **Sunshine Early Learning Center**, a childcare facility that faced serious challenges due to non-compliance with regulations. Sunshine was a thriving facility in a busy urban neighborhood, but the owner, Sarah, had not paid enough attention to the ever-evolving regulations governing childcare in her state.

One day, during a routine inspection by the state childcare regulatory agency, Sarah was informed that her facility was not in compliance with several key regulations, including child-to-staff ratios and staff certification requirements. The inspector noted that some of the staff members were not up-to-date on required first-aid training, and the facility lacked documentation proving that background checks had been conducted for all staff members.

As a result of these violations, Sarah faced fines, an action plan with deadlines for correcting the issues, and a temporary suspension of enrollment for new children. Although Sarah immediately addressed the issues by hiring additional staff and completing the required training, the damage to the facility's reputation was significant. Parents were concerned, and some chose to withdraw their children from the center. In addition, the cost of rectifying these issues—hiring new staff, conducting background checks, and providing the necessary training—was financially burdensome.

This experience served as a harsh reminder of the importance of compliance. Had Sarah stayed ahead of regulatory changes and kept a closer eye on the requirements, the facility could have avoided these setbacks. Instead, she learned the hard way that compliance is not optional but a fundamental part of running a trustworthy and reputable childcare business.

Steps to Ensure Compliance

To avoid the pitfalls that Sarah encountered and ensure your business remains in compliance, follow these practical steps:

1. Stay Informed About Local and State Regulations

- Laws and regulations related to childcare can change frequently, so it's essential to stay informed about the specific rules that apply to your facility. Sign up for newsletters, attend local childcare provider meetings, and check with your state's childcare licensing agency regularly to stay up to date on new laws and regulations.

2. Implement Comprehensive Policies and Procedures

- Develop written policies and procedures that clearly outline how your facility will meet compliance standards in all areas, from staff qualifications to safety protocols. Make sure these policies are regularly reviewed and updated to reflect any regulatory changes.

3. Conduct Regular Training for Staff

- Regular training is essential for ensuring that your team understands and adheres to compliance requirements. This includes not only required certifications (e.g., CPR, first aid) but also training on child safety, developmentally appropriate practices, and emergency response protocols.

4. Maintain Accurate Records

- Keep detailed records of everything related to compliance—staff certifications, training schedules, background checks, and incident reports. A well-organized filing system will ensure that you can quickly provide documentation during inspections or audits.

5. Monitor Staff-to-Child Ratios

- One of the most critical regulations is maintaining appropriate child-to-staff ratios. Regularly check your staffing levels and adjust as needed to ensure that you are meeting these requirements. Keep a daily log of the children in attendance and the staff present to make sure you are compliant at all times.

6. Prepare for Inspections

- Inspections are a routine part of childcare licensing, so it's important to be prepared. Conduct internal audits and mock inspections to identify areas that may need improvement. This proactive approach will help you pass inspections with ease and avoid surprises.

7. Foster Transparency with Parents

- Open communication with parents is a key element of compliance. Ensure that parents are informed about your policies, their children's progress, and any changes to your facility. This will not only help you build trust but also ensure that parents understand their rights and your obligations under the law.

Tools to Help You Stay Compliant

There are several tools and resources available that can help you maintain compliance and stay organized:

- **Childcare Management Software**: Platforms like Procare and Kinderlime can help you track children's attendance, staff hours, and even communicate with parents. These tools often come with built-in compliance features that make it easier to meet licensing requirements.

- **Compliance Checklists**: Create or download comprehensive compliance checklists that cover all regulatory areas for your state. These can help you ensure that you're meeting all necessary requirements.

- **Employee Training Platforms**: Websites like Care Courses or Red Cross offer online training programs that can help your staff stay up-to-date on certifications such as first aid and CPR.

The Benefits of Compliance

The benefits of maintaining compliance go far beyond just avoiding fines or penalties. When your facility is compliant, it signals to parents and the community that you take your responsibilities seriously and that the safety and well-being of the children are your top priorities. Here are some key advantages:

- **Building Trust with Parents**: Parents are more likely to trust your facility if they know that you are meeting all legal and regulatory requirements. This trust can translate into increased enrollment and long-term relationships.

- **Fostering a Safe and Secure Environment**: Compliance ensures that your facility is safe and that children are cared for in a healthy, supportive environment.

- **Reputation Management**: A childcare facility with a strong track record of compliance has a positive reputation in the community, which can lead to more referrals and a steady flow of clients.

- **Reduced Risk of Legal Issues**: By meeting compliance requirements, you reduce the risk of lawsuits, fines, and other legal issues that can arise from negligence or failure to comply.

Conclusion: Compliance is Key to Quality Childcare

In the childcare industry, compliance is non-negotiable. It's essential not only for the safety and well-being of the children in your care but also for the long-term success of your business. By staying informed, maintaining accurate records, and implementing effective policies and procedures, you can ensure that your facility meets all legal requirements and provides the highest quality care possible.

Compliance isn't just about meeting the bare minimum standards; it's about going above and beyond to create an environment where children can thrive, parents feel secure, and staff are empowered to do their best work. By committing to compliance, you're making an investment in the future of your childcare business—and the children you serve.

- Childcare Guru

PART FIVE

Challenges & Commitments

Commitments – The Road to Success and Resilience in Childcare

There's so much glory in the story of building a childcare business from the ground up, but behind that glory lies a journey filled with challenges, tough decisions, and sacrifices. As you venture into the childcare industry, it's essential to understand that the path to success requires more than just a passion for caring for children. It requires commitment—commitment to growth, to facing obstacles head-on, and to constantly adapting to ensure your business thrives, even when things get tough.

In this chapter, I want to share the commitments that fueled my journey, the lessons I learned along the way, and the strategies I used to position myself for success. I hope this story inspires you, and most importantly, prepares you for the challenges you may face as you build and grow your childcare business.

The Early Days: From One Minivan to a Growing Business

When I first started my childcare journey, I didn't have much. I started my daycare in my home, with a minivan I purchased for $900. The van had only one working side, but it was all I could afford. At the time, I was licensed for 10 children, and I made sure to fill that capacity every single day. It wasn't glamorous, and it wasn't easy, but I was committed to giving my all to the children and families who trusted me.

I used grassroots marketing to attract clients—passing out flyers, knocking on doors, and doing everything I could to build a clientele. It wasn't instant success, but I stuck with it. Every step forward, no matter how small, was a victory. After 9 months, I moved into my first official center. I was now licensed for 21 children, but I had to start all over to build new relationships and credibility in the community. Only three families from my original group followed me, and I had to work tirelessly to attract new families.

I knew I was on the right path, but I also understood that success would not come without hard work, perseverance, and, most importantly, patience. The early years were full of sacrifice, but every obstacle became an opportunity for growth.

Expanding the Vision: From One Location to Multiple Centers

After three years, I opened my second center in Orange Park, licensed for 45 children. The marketing tactics I had relied on—passing out flyers—didn't work as effectively in the new area. I had to pivot. I started advertising on the radio, in local magazines, and at restaurants. I showed up at festivals, schools, and community events. I made sure my brand was visible at every turn.

It took nine months to fill the new center. I learned quickly that visibility was key to building trust. I couldn't just expect families to find me; I had to make my presence known and show up consistently. By getting involved in the community and engaging with local families, I was able to build the reputation and trust that I needed to grow my business.

Setbacks and Resilience: Learning from the Starke Experience

As my business expanded, I decided to open a third location in Starke, Florida. This facility was much larger than my previous centers, spanning 5,000 square feet. The previous owners had marketed it as a daycare and private school, but after six months of operating, I realized this was not a viable business move. The community was very tight-knit, and it was hard for newcomers to break in. I learned a tough lesson: not every opportunity is the right one, and sometimes, walking away is the best choice.

It was a setback, but I didn't let it define me. Instead of seeing it as a failure, I decided to learn from it and shift my focus. I went back to the drawing board and launched a daycare staffing agency. My experience of struggling to find reliable staff inspired me to train and mentor others in the childcare industry. I taught teachers how to be effective childcare professionals, and I contracted them out to other facilities. This was a new venture, and it thrived because I recognized a gap in the industry that no one was addressing—providing quality training for daycare staff.

A Dream Becomes Reality: Investing in Property

While I was growing my staffing agency, I had my eye on two buildings side by side that I drove by every day. The thought of owning those buildings felt like a distant dream. I never thought I'd be approved for a loan to purchase them, especially since my financial situation wasn't ideal. But after driving past the buildings one day and noticing the "For Sale" signs had disappeared, I panicked. I called my mom for advice, and she encouraged me to call the realtor. To my surprise, the buildings were still available.

I called the realtor and made an appointment to view the properties, despite having no approval for financing and no money to speak of. The buildings needed significant work, and I was uncertain about how I could make it happen. But I decided to take the leap and move forward anyway. After meeting with the bank and being turned away, I was referred to another lender. The process was stressful, and when the lender called me back with approval, I was in disbelief.

I had to come up with 20% for the down payment, and while I was only able to purchase one building in May, it wasn't until October that I was able to secure the second one. The remodeling process took a year, and just as I was wrapping up the final touches, the pandemic hit.

Surviving the Pandemic: Resilience and Innovation

The pandemic hit hard. Our enrollment numbers dropped from 100 children to just 25. I had three sets of bills to pay—my home and two buildings—while my income plummeted. My sister was the only employee who stayed with me, and we were forced to scale back operations. But we remained committed. We kept the faith, even when the outlook seemed bleak. We went back to the drawing board and taught ourselves how to adapt to the new circumstances.

We implemented new health-conscious practices, including masks, sanitizing protocols, and individual supplies for each child. Slowly, as the restrictions lifted, parents returned. Many were working from home, and we had to find ways to accommodate their needs. We implemented flexible schedules, and as families adjusted, we adapted our services to provide the support they needed.

The Commitment to Never Giving Up

Throughout all of these challenges, the one thing that kept me going was my commitment to the children, the families, and the staff who believed in me. There were countless times when I wanted to give up, when the financial strain, the stress, and the uncertainty seemed too much to bear. But every time I felt that way, I would remind myself of why I started this journey in the first place: to make a positive impact on the lives of children and to build a business that would support future generations.

When you're committed to something greater than yourself, you find the strength to keep going, even when the road is tough. It's about pushing through the difficult moments and knowing that your efforts are not in vain. The journey isn't always smooth, but it's always worth it.

Wrapping Up: Your Journey, Your Commitment

Building a childcare business isn't easy. It requires unwavering commitment, the ability to adapt to changing circumstances, and the resilience to overcome setbacks. The road to success is not linear, but with each challenge, you learn, grow, and move closer to your vision.

As you embark on your own journey in the childcare industry, remember that commitment is key. Stay focused on your mission, be prepared to face obstacles, and never lose sight of the impact you want to make. You have the power to create something truly special—a childcare facility that not only meets the needs of the children and families you serve but also contributes to the betterment of your community.

The road ahead will have its ups and downs, but with commitment, perseverance, and a clear vision, you can overcome any challenge and build a thriving childcare business that makes a lasting impact.